RAND NATIONAL DEFENSE RESEARCH INSTITUTE

T0302935

Elements of Success

How Type of Secondary Education Credential Helps Predict Enlistee Attrition

Susan Burkhauser, Lawrence M. Hanser, Chaitra M. Hardison

Prepared for the Office of the Secretary of Defense
Approved for public release; distribution unlimited

The research described in this report was prepared for the Office of the Secretary of Defense (OSD). The research was conducted within the RAND National Defense Research Institute, a federally funded research and development center sponsored by OSD, the Joint Staff, the Unified Combatant Commands, the Navy, the Marine Corps, the defense agencies, and the defense Intelligence Community under Contract W74V8H-06-C-0002.

Library of Congress Cataloging-in-Publication Data is available for this publication.

ISBN: 978-0-8330-8424-8

RAND OFFICES

SANTA MONICA, CA • WASHINGTON, DC

PITTSBURGH, PA • NEW ORLEANS, LA • JACKSON, MS • BOSTON, MA

DOHA, QA • CAMBRIDGE, UK • BRUSSELS, BE

www.rand.org

Preface

Aptitude for successful military service in the enlisted ranks includes the ability to succeed in at least one of many military occupational specialties, career fields, or ratings and the ability to adapt to and thrive in a military lifestyle of good order and discipline. The Department of Defense screens military applicants for these qualities using the Armed Forces Qualification Test from the Armed Services Vocational Aptitude Battery, physical and moral standards, and educational credentials. Historically, educational credentials have served as a proxy for the ability to adapt to a military lifestyle. Evidence that supports this use is the stark difference in completion rates for the initial term of service between recruits who hold traditional high school diplomas and those who hold General Educational Development certificates. However, the last few decades have witnessed an explosion of ways to earn education credentials, including homeschooling and distance learning. Therefore, at this juncture, it is important to consider whether these particular education credentials (specifically those for homeschool and distance learning) remain suitable proxies for predicting first-term attrition. This report examines whether the current use of the education tiers better predicts first-term attrition rates than not using education credential information at all. The results should be of interest to Congress and Department of Defense policymakers who set policies for entrance into enlisted military service, as well as to the military services' recruiting services.

This research was sponsored by the Director of Accession Policy in the Office of the Undersecretary of Defense for Personnel and Readiness and conducted within the Forces and Resources Policy Center of RAND's National Defense Research Institute, a federally funded research and development center sponsored by the Office of the Secretary of Defense, the Joint Staff, the Unified Combatant Commands, the Navy, the Marine Corps, the defense agencies, and the defense Intelligence Community. For more information on the RAND Forces and Resources Policy Center, see http://www.rand.org/nsrd/ndri/centers/frp.html or contact the director (contact information is provided on the web page).

Contents

Figures

Tables

Acknowledgments

This project would not have been possible without our sponsor, Jane Arabian, Assistant Director, Accession Policy, Office of the Under Secretary of Defense (Personnel and Readiness). We would also like to thank Marisa Michaels, Matthew Plumb, Scott Seggerman, and Richard Moreno of DMDC for their help in procuring the data used in this report.

Judy Mele at RAND helped prepare and offered guidance on the data. Lou Mariano provided feedback on early analysis work. We also are grateful for the efforts of our internal and external reviewers, Jennifer Lamping Lewis, Trey Miller, Jennie Wegner, and Shanthi Nataraj, whose thoughtful comments resulted in numerous improvements to the final report.

Abbreviations

AFQT	Armed Forces Qualification Test
DMDC	Defense Manpower Data Center
DoD	Department of Defense
FY	fiscal year
GED	General Educational Development certificate
MEPCOM	Military Entrance Processing Command
OSD	Office of the Undersecretary of Defense

CHAPTER ONE

Introduction

Education credentials in combination with Armed Forces Qualification Test (AFQT) scores (derived from the Armed Services Vocational Aptitude Battery) are the primary elements the U.S. military services use to define enlisted recruit quality. AFQT scores have traditionally been used to predict performance in training and on the job. In contrast, education credentials have traditionally been used to identify candidates who are more likely to attrit during the first term of service. Prior to 2012, three groupings, or tiers, were used to define education credentials. The top tier (Tier 1) consisted of three broad groups: traditional high school diplomas, completion of some college, and an adult education diploma. The second tier (Tier 2) consisted of two broad groups: equivalency credentials (the General Educational Development certificate [GED]) and other alternative high school credentials (e.g., distance learning or virtual diplomas). The third tier (Tier 3) comprised non–high school graduates. The three tier groupings were established on the basis of past research identifying the types of credentials generally associated with a higher risk of attrition than traditional high school diplomas. Because the base rates of new and alternative forms of education credentials (e.g., distance learning or virtual and homeschooling) have been low in the past, very few data have been available to guide the Office of the Secretary of Defense's (OSD's) categorization of these alternative forms. At present, however, the services have amassed enough data to permit further examination of these alternative credentials.

Two credentials of particular interest for Department of Defense (DoD) policy are homeschooling and distance learning or virtual schooling. As noted above, for several years prior to 2012, DoD classified homeschool diplomas and distance learning or virtual school diplomas as Tier 2 credentials.[1] The 2012 National Defense Authorization Act (H. R. 1540) changed that by mandating that OSD treat recruits holding such diplomas as covered graduates and classify them as Tier 1 when the recruit has also obtained scores on other factors (such as aptitude or personality test scores) that are known to be associated with lower attrition or an increased ability to adapt to military life.[2] The act left it to OSD to define the factors to be used in combination with the credential to elevate covered graduates to Tier 1. OSD implemented the mandate in June 2012 and provided the services with the following guidelines (Vollrath, 2012):

> covered graduates with AFQT scores at or above 50 (AFQT Categories I–IIIA) will be given the same enlistment priority (Tier 1) as traditional high school diploma gradu-

[1] Homeschooling degrees were classified as Tier 1 from 1999–2004.

[2] The 2012 National Defense Authorization Act defines a *covered graduate* as someone who has received a diploma from a legally operating secondary school or who has otherwise completed a program of secondary education in compliance with the laws of the state in which the person resides.

ates and will be counted as such in recruit quality reporting. Covered graduates with lower AFQT scores may still be enlisted with lower priority (Tier 2) at Military Service discretion.

OSD asked RAND to assist in determining whether analyses of existing attrition data support continued use of this approach.

Study Approach

We responded to OSD's request in two ways. First, we asked the following narrowly focused research question to determine whether existing attrition data support the current policy regarding distance learning and homeschool credentials: Are applicants with less than 50 on the AFQT who have distance learning or homeschool credentials more likely to attrit within the first three years than those with high school diplomas (all else being equal)?[3]

Second, we asked a broader research question: What is known about education credentials, and how could OSD's education credentialing policy be improved?

This project report summarizes only the results pertaining to the first, narrowly focused research question. The work addressing the second question will be described in a separate report.

Addressing the First Narrowly Focused Research Question

To address the first research question, we compared attrition rates for enlistees holding four types of education credentials:

- high school diploma
- test-based equivalency diploma (such as a GED)
- homeschool diploma
- distance learning or virtual school diploma (hereafter referred to simply as distance learning).

We obtained individual-level data through the Defense Manpower Data Center (DMDC) on all personnel who enlisted from years 2000 through 2012 for use in our attrition analyses.[4] Education credential type, AFQT scores, dates of entry, and dates of separation were the core variables we requested from DMDC. We also requested data elements that covered a wide variety of demographic variables, such as race, gender, and occupational specialty, to allow us to control for any observable demographic differences between the types of people holding each education credential.

To answer our research question, we first calculated raw attrition rates by education credential and AFQT score. Then, we applied two statistical regression techniques to control for

---

[3] Predicting attrition is the stated purpose for OSD's education credential tier policy. We therefore focus on attrition as the outcome of interest in these analyses.

[4] We used DMDC's Military Entrance Processing Command (MEPCOM) and Active Duty Military Personnel edit files in these analyses.

observable population characteristics across credential groups when computing attrition rates. The first was a propensity score analysis that statistically balances the groups prior to calculating the group's predicted attrition rates through logistic regression. The second was a simple unweighted logistic regression approach. The results of both methods produce similar results; therefore, we present only the propensity score analyses in the body of the report.

Organization of This Report

The remainder of this report presents our attrition analyses. In Chapter Two, we start with an overview of the variables we used and key data limitations. We then present raw attrition rates by education credential and AFQT score. We next describe the statistical methodology we used to examine differences in attrition rates across the education credential groups. Chapter Three provides our statistical results and our major conclusions regarding the usefulness of the current education credential policy.

Four appendices provide additional technical information to support the analyses described in the text. Appendix A provides descriptive statistics for key study variables. Appendix B compares the unweighted sample means to the propensity score weighted sample means on each demographic variable included in the propensity score models. Appendix C describes the models for the main regression analysis. Appendix D describes the simple logistic regression models we used to supplement the propensity score findings.

CHAPTER TWO

Attrition Analyses

This chapter provides an overview of the data and of the statistical methods used to examine attrition.

Data

Overview

Altogether, the military services enlist over 300,000 individuals per year, but fewer than 0.5 percent of these individuals have homeschool diplomas and 0.1 percent or fewer have distance learning diplomas at enlistment. This meant that we would have to include several cohorts of accessions to obtain a reasonable sample of individuals with these characteristics to analyze. As a result, we sought to obtain data on regular non–prior service enlisted accessions who could have completed at least 12 months of service. We received data from DMDC from the MEPCOM Edit File, which contained information for persons who were accessed from 2000 to 2012,[1] and from the Active Duty Military Personnel Edit File, which contained information for each active duty enlisted person who was accessed from 2000 to 2012 and the most recent data on all enlisted personnel who were in the service between 2000 and 2012, regardless of their accession date and regardless of whether or not they have separated.[2]

Following DMDC practice, we used the MEPCOM file as the basis for determining who was accessed during the time frame of interest. This file also provided demographic data, education credential, and AFQT score. We then merged this file with the active duty file to obtain career information (i.e., occupation code, months of active service, separation date). Figure 2.1 shows how we narrowed this sample down to a final sample of 1,999,459 enlisted personnel. In short, this sample includes all enlisted personnel who at the time of the creation of the original dataset were regular active duty, non–prior service, nonprisoner, and who had enlisted during fiscal years 2000 through 2011.[3] Our analyses were completed on different relevant subsets of this sample of 1,999,459, so sample sizes will differ for different analyses. For example, not

[1] This data file contains data collected at the MEPCOM at the time of accession (e.g., AFQT score, education credential, home of record, zip code, marital status).

[2] This data file contains military service career data that are updated throughout a service member's career (e.g., duty DoD occupation code, marital status, home of record). These data present a snapshot of what is true about the service member as of the file date. We received both a master file with data on all enlisted personnel and a transaction file with accessed separation profiles, which contained the same variables as the master file and included additional variables related to separation.

[3] Although we received data on persons who were accessed in FY 2012, our attrition analysis did not include them because their tenure was too short.

Figure 2.1
Process of Selecting Observations for Analysis

Total accessions	3,253,131
Non–regular service accessions	- 921,123
Prior service accessions	- 133,310
Accessions after FY 2011	- 140,757
Accessions with no record in the active duty file	- 34,799
Accessions with active duty file dates earlier than their MEPCOM file dates	- 16,588
Accessions with officer pay grade or officer occupation code	- 5,193
Prisoners	- 1,902
Observations used in final data set	1,999,459

SOURCES: DMDC MEPCOM and Active Duty Military Personnel edit files.
RAND *RR374-2.1*

all 1,999,459 individuals had been enlisted long enough to have served 36 months, so our analysis of 36-month attrition excluded those who had not. Throughout the remainder of this report, we describe how we chose the subset of individuals for each analysis, starting from these 1,999,459 individuals.

Descriptive Statistics

Figure 2.2 shows the trends in 12-, 24-, and 36-month attrition rates for entering cohorts FYs 2000–2011 by service.[4]

Table 2.1 shows the percentage of enlistees by education credential at the time of accession and AFQT category. We see that practically no enlistees have an AFQT less than or equal to 30 (categories IVA to V).

Table 2.2 shows the percentage of enlistees by their education credential at the time of accession and by service. In each service, the vast majority of enlistees have a traditional high school diploma; the Army has the lowest percentage (70.1 percent), the Air Force the highest (92.9 percent). The next highest category for all services is Other Tier 1 Credential; fewer than 1 percent of enlistees in each service from FYs 2000 to 2011 had a homeschool or distance learning school diploma.

Table 2.3 shows the percentage of enlistees by their education credential at the time of accession and by entry cohort. In general, the proportion of enlistees with each credential type has stayed fairly stable over time. The one noticeable difference is in the trend for enlistees with GEDs, which increased until the FY 2008 cohort. After this, there was a large drop, from 10 percent to 4.5 percent in FY 2009, and a drop to about 1 percent in FY 2011. One hypothesis for this drop is that the economic recession resulted in fewer job opportunities and a higher demand for military enlistment; the military thus did not need to enlist as many Tier 2 applicants. This hypothesis is supported by the increase in high school diplomas and other Tier 1 credentials over the same period. This is something we plan to investigate further in our second project report.

---

[4] Attrition within a given number of months is defined as a separation from the military and an active federal military service month value less than that number of months. See Appendix A for tables detailing the data.

Figure 2.2
Raw Attrition Rates by Service and Entry Cohort FY

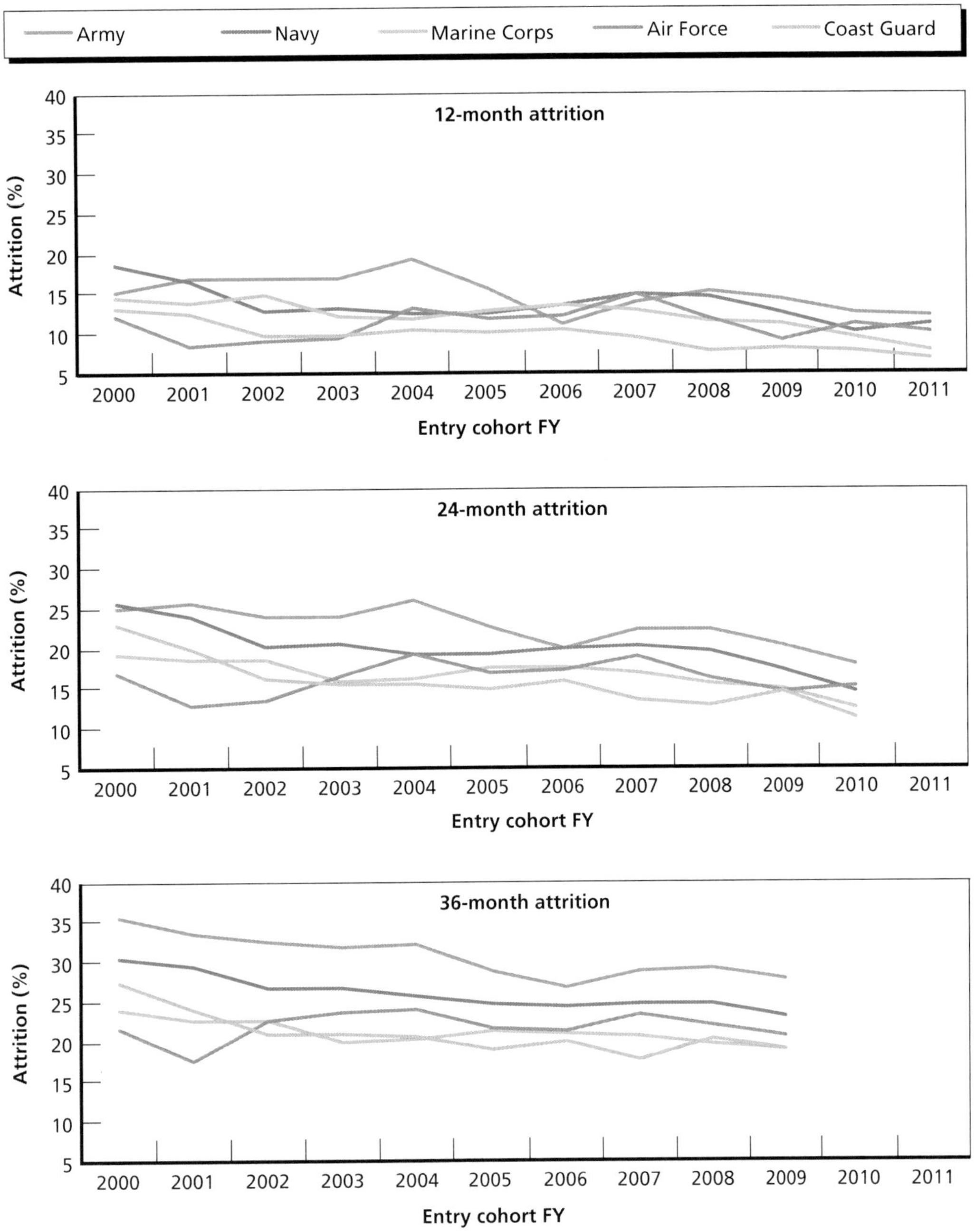

SOURCES: DMDC MEPCOM and Active Duty Military Personnel edit files.
RAND *RR374-2.2*

Data Limitations

We encountered a few notable limitations while working with the data. One is the unknown reason for the drop in enlistees with GED credentials from 2008 to 2011. A second is that enlistees with Tier 2 or Tier 3 (less than high school) credentials are generally required to

Table 2.1
Distribution of Accession Education Credential by AFQT Category Code

AFQT Category	High School Diploma (%)	Homeschool Diploma (%)	Distance Learning School Diploma (%)	GED (%)	Less than High School Diploma (%)	Other Tier 1 Credential (%)	Other Tier 2 Credential (%)
I (AFQT>92)	5.1	6.4	4.0	1.7	1.7	14.9	1.2
II (92≥AFQT≥65)	37.2	40.5	37.1	32.3	34.5	41.6	20.7
IIIA (64≥AFQT≥50)	27.0	28.9	38.8	40.1	51.3	20.4	28.6
IIIB (49≥AFQT≥31)	29.5	23.7	19.8	25.7	12.4	22.2	47.2
IVA (30≥AFQT≥21)	1.1	0.5	0.2	0.1	0.0	0.9	2.1
IVB (20≥AFQT≥16)	0.0	0.0	0.0	0.0	0.0	0.0	0.0
IVC (15≥AFQT≥10)	0.0	0.0	0.0	0.0	0.0	0.0	0.0
V (AFQT<10)	0.0	0.0	0.0	0.0	0.0	0.0	0.0

SOURCES: DMDC MEPCOM and Active Duty Military Personnel edit files.

NOTE: Other Tier 1 credentials include some college, postsecondary school or greater, current high school senior, high school graduate who failed the exit exam, and adult education diploma. Other Tier 2 credentials include ChalleNGe GED, high school certificate of attendance, and occupational program.

Table 2.2
Distribution of Accession Education Credential by Service

Service	High School Diploma (%)	Homeschool Diploma (%)	Distance Learning School Diploma (%)	GED (%)	Less than High School Diploma (%)	Other Tier 1 Credential (%)	Other Tier 2 Credential (%)
Army	70.1	0.5	0.0	13.2	0.9	13.7	1.6
Navy	85.2	0.4	0.1	3.4	1.8	8.5	0.6
Marine Corps	91.8	0.7	0.1	1.8	0.2	4.8	0.7
Air Force	92.9	0.2	0.0	0.4	0.1	6.3	0.1
Coast Guard	84.0	0.2	0.0	5.5	0.0	10.2	0.1

SOURCES: DMDC MEPCOM and Active Duty Military Personnel edit files.

NOTE: Other Tier 1 credentials include some college, postsecondary school or greater, current high school senior, high school graduate who failed the exit exam, and adult education diploma. Other Tier 2 credentials include ChalleNGe GED, high school certificate of attendance, and occupational program.

Table 2.3
Distribution of Accession Education Credential by Entry Cohort FYs

Entry Cohort (FY)	High School Diploma	Homeschool Diploma	Distance Learning School Diploma	GED	Less than High School Diploma	Other Tier 1 Credential	Other Tier 2 Credential
2000	84.4	0.4	0.0	6.9	1.2	6.5	0.6
2001	82.4	0.5	0.0	7.9	1.1	7.3	0.7
2002	82.6	0.4	0.0	6.7	0.8	8.4	1.0
2003	84.2	0.3	0.0	5.4	0.5	8.5	1.0
2004	82.6	0.4	0.0	5.1	0.5	10.1	1.3
2005	80.7	0.5	0.1	7.2	0.3	10.2	1.1
2006	77.4	0.4	0.1	10.3	1.2	9.7	0.8
2007	76.3	0.5	0.1	10.9	1.4	9.6	1.2
2008	78.5	0.6	0.2	10.0	0.7	8.8	1.1
2009	82.2	0.5	0.1	4.5	1.5	10.3	0.9
2010	85.4	0.5	0.0	1.0	0.2	12.3	0.6
2011	85.1	0.4	0.0	0.7	0.0	13.2	0.5

SOURCES: DMDC MEPCOM and Active Duty Military Personnel edit files.

NOTE: Other Tier 1 credentials include some college, postsecondary school or greater, current high school senior, high school graduate who failed the exit exam, and adult education diploma. Other Tier 2 credentials include ChalleNGe GED, high school certificate of attendance, and occupational program.

attain AFQT scores of at least 50. However, as Table 2.1 shows, a substantial percentage of enlistees with Tier 2 and Tier 3 credentials have scores below 50: 24 percent of those with homeschool diplomas (N = 2,162), 20 percent of those with distance learning school diplomas (N = 245), 26 percent of those with GEDs (N = 32,841), 49 percent of those with different Tier 2 credentials (N = 8,774), and 13 percent of those with less than high school (N = 1,969). It is still possible to enlist with lower AFQT scores with a waiver. Performing the same breakdown on only accessions without waivers for "mental qualification—meets ASVAB testing requirements" (see Appendix A) produces similar results for all Tier 2 and Tier 3 credentials: 24 percent of those with homeschool diplomas (N = 2,150), 20 percent of those with distance learning school diplomas (N = 244), 26 percent of those with GEDs (N = 32,731), 49 percent of those with different Tier 2 credentials (N = 8,744), and 13 percent of those with less than high school (N = 1,964). One additional alternative we are aware of is that homeschool diplomas were classified as Tier 1 from 1999 through 2004, so any scores below 50 would not have needed a waiver for this education credential during that time. However, breaking down the data to show percentage of enlistees with AFQT scores greater or equal to 50 by year of enlistment and education credential, as shown in Table 2.4, does not show that this is the source of the discrepancy. It is possible that some of those who scored below 50 provided the

Table 2.4
Percentage of Enlistees with AFQT Scores of 50 or Greater by Accession Education Credential and Entry Cohort FYs

Entry Cohort FYs	High School Diploma	Homeschool Diploma	Distance Learning School Diploma	GED	Less than High School Diploma	Other Tier 1 Credential	Other Tier 2 Credential
2000	64.8	57.0	70.0	82.4	96.8	66.1	48.8
2001	65.5	58.7	80.8	71.9	97.3	68.0	44.5
2002	67.9	68.5	90.8	86.5	98.1	72.1	44.1
2003	70.0	71.5	98.7	96.9	95.3	77.2	49.6
2004	71.5	70.6	85.5	85.3	97.1	82.1	47.0
2005	69.5	70.1	74.2	65.4	95.8	80.3	46.8
2006	68.5	67.6	71.3	60.8	62.1	77.5	41.6
2007	67.6	74.3	72.0	61.3	61.8	76.4	53.3
2008	67.8	80.1	73.8	66.4	91.9	74.8	56.1
2009	70.5	92.2	88.4	86.6	99.2	78.3	64.9
2010	73.1	98.1	91.5	98.4	95.9	80.3	58.4
2011	76.5	98.2	100.0	99.1	87.5	82.6	58.4

SOURCES: DMDC MEPCOM and Active Duty Military Personnel edit files.

NOTE: Other Tier 1 credentials include some college, postsecondary school or greater, current high school senior, high school graduate who failed the exit exam, and adult education diploma. Other Tier 2 credentials include ChalleNGe GED, high school certificate of attendance, and occupational program.

services a Tier 1 credential at a later date, after applying but before enlisting, and that their files were never updated to reflect the new credential.[5]

Raw Attrition Rates by Education Credential and AFQT Score

Table 2.5 displays raw attrition rates by length of service and education credential. For all periods, homeschool diploma recipients and distance learning school diploma recipients had higher attrition rates than traditional high school diploma recipients did.

Table 2.6 provides a further examination of raw attrition rates by education credential by comparing attrition rates for those with AFQT scores greater than or equal to 50 to those with AFQT scores below 50, the score that currently triggers differential acceptance based on education credential. This table provides some insight on why it might make sense to consider an applicant's AFQT score in combination with his or her education credential; a homeschool diploma recipient with less than 50 on the AFQT has 12-, 24-, and 36-month attrition rates that are 9, 12, and 13 percentage points higher, respectively, than the rates for a homeschool

[5] This could in part explain the number of personnel who were enlisted with less than a high school diploma. Perhaps they were in the process of obtaining high school diplomas (e.g., they had applied during their senior year) when the education credential information was entered. They could have been logged as having no high school diploma at that time. The services may then have subsequently enlisted them when they showed proof of completing the degree but may not have updated the education credential code. This is purely supposition; we have no concrete explanation for why the number of enlistees with no high school credential is so large. Nevertheless, we do suggest that the services take steps to check that the education credential admission records are being updated when applicants' education credential has changed prior to being enlisted. Doing so will help alleviate some of the concerns about data accuracy that we have raised here.

Table 2.5
Raw Attrition Rates

Period	Credential	Total	Attrition (%)
12-month attrition	High school diploma	1,617,493	13
	Homeschool diploma	8,917	18
	Distance learning school diploma	1,222	19
	GED	127,624	21
24-month attrition	High school diploma	1,489,367	19
	Homeschool diploma	8,247	26
	Distance learning school diploma	1,176	28
	GED	126,560	32
36-month attrition	High school diploma	1,358,615	25
	Homeschool diploma	7,525	34
	Distance learning school diploma	1117	34
	GED	125,102	40

SOURCE: DMDC MEPCOM and Active Duty Military Personnel edit files.

NOTE: Table includes only non–prior service accessions. Twelve-month attrition includes fiscal years (FYs) 2000–2011; 24-month attrition includes FYs 2000–2010; and 36-month attrition includes FYs 2000–2009. Services represented are Army, Navy, Marine Corps, Air Force, and Coast Guard.

Table 2.6
Raw Attrition Rates by AFQT Category

		AFQT >= 50 (I to IIIA)		AFQT < 50 (IIIB to V)	
Period	Credential	Total	Attrition (%)	Total	Attrition (%)
12-month attrition	High school diploma	1,119,444	12	494,970	14
	Homeschool diploma	6,745	15	2,162	24
	Distance learning school diploma	976	19	245	21
	GED	94,441	22	32,841	21
24-month attrition	High school diploma	1,021,479	17	464,895	21
	Homeschool diploma	6,088	23	2,150	35
	Distance learning school diploma	930	27	245	31
	GED	93,393	32	32,831	32
36-month attrition	High school diploma	926,009	23	429,712	27
	Homeschool diploma	5,380	30	2,136	43
	Distance learning school diploma	876	33	240	39
	GED	91,962	40	32,808	41

SOURCES: DMDC MEPCOM and Active Duty Military Personnel edit files.

NOTE: Table includes only non–prior service accessions. Twelve-month attrition includes FYs 2000–2011; 24-month attrition includes FYs 2000–2010; and 36-month attrition includes FYs 2000–2009. Services represented are Army, Navy, Marine Corps, Air Force, and Coast Guard.

diploma recipient with more than 50 on the AFQT. The pattern is similar for all education credentials; however, the difference is largest for homeschool diploma and distance learning school diploma for each period.

However, drawing conclusions based on an examination of raw attrition rates can be misleading. For example, if recruits with homeschool diplomas tend to enter occupations that themselves exhibit high attrition rates, while recruits with regular high school diplomas tend to enter occupations with low attrition rates, the differences we observe in simple raw attrition rates may be a function of the occupations entered and unrelated to education credential. More-sophisticated analysis techniques, as described below, can help isolate the attrition differences that are due to education credential alone.

Statistical Methodology

If two applicants for military service are the same in all characteristics except that one has a regular high school diploma and the other has a different kind of high school credential, such as a GED, is there sufficient reason to treat them differently in terms of enlistment standards? One primary difficulty in addressing the question of whether education credential itself leads to an increased likelihood of attrition is the issue of causality. In an ideal world, we would identify the causal effect of education credentials on attrition by conducting a double-blind, randomized experiment in which individuals would be randomly assigned to attend high school, obtain a GED, be homeschooled, or complete a diploma via distance learning. However, such an experiment is not feasible for studying the impact of an education credential—parents, or parents and children together, choose which education credential to obtain. Instead, the data available to answer this question are observational. That is, people have decided for themselves (or their parents decided) which education credential they would receive, and we can only observe what they decided and the resulting military service outcomes. An examination of raw attrition rates for these groups is therefore particularly misleading with respect to inferences of causality because of the role of these possible self-selection confounds.

Instead, more-sophisticated statistical analysis techniques are needed to help disentangle some of these possible confounds. One traditional technique is to use simple linear regression models with covariates to control for model identification problems, such as omitted variable bias. We report the results of this traditional technique in Appendix D. Doubly robust propensity weighted regression models include covariates in the same way that simple regressions models do but include additional steps toward estimating the causal effect of education credential on attrition. Although this still does not permit a strict test of causality, it does create a closer approximation of what the outcomes for the groups of interest might look like if we were to conduct a traditional experiment with random assignment.

Doubly robust propensity weighted regression techniques offer a number of advantages over traditional regression approaches to understanding the influence of a predictor variable (such as education credential) on a later organizational outcome (such as attrition). They nevertheless share many of the same limitations as traditional regression. One major limitation is the possibility of omitted variables. Covariates that are omitted from either simple linear regression models or doubly robust propensity weighted regression could affect our findings in ways that cannot be anticipated. For that reason, we asked DMDC for a wide variety of demographic variables and included them as controls in the regressions provided here.[6] This technique is explained in detail below, and we present the results of this technique in Chapter Three.

Doubly Robust Propensity Weighted Regression Analyses

Historically, the military services have treated applicants with high school diplomas differently from applicants with GEDs because recruits with GEDs have much higher attrition rates. We sought to compare the attrition rates of recruits who have either a homeschool or distance learning diploma with recruits who have either a regular high school diploma or a GED. We used doubly robust estimation techniques, including propensity weights and regression, to control for nonrandom assignment of education credential status in comparing 12-, 24-, and 36-month attrition rates.[7] The doubly robust propensity weighted regression analyses attempted to control for a number of confounding variables (e.g., specific military service entered, entry-year cohort, occupational specialty, race or ethnicity, and gender) that are related to the variable of interest (i.e., education credential) and to attrition.

This technique requires estimating two models. First, we computed a *propensity score* for each member of the comparison group using a logistic regression. We computed four regressions of education credential (i.e., homeschool versus regular diploma, homeschool versus GED, distance learning versus regular diploma, and distance learning versus GED) on the vector of observable characteristics (demographics, AFQT, occupational codes, etc.).[8] The predictions from these models created the propensity scores. This propensity score is the predicted probability of each member of each comparison group (i.e., recruits with regular high school diplomas and recruits with GEDs) having the education credential of interest (homeschool or distance learning diplomas), conditional on the observable characteristics (e.g., specific military service entered, entry cohort, occupational code, race or ethnicity, and gender).[9] The propensity scores indicate the similarity between each comparison group member and a typical recruit with a homeschool or distance learning diploma. Adjusting for the propensity scores in the analyses of attrition probability using propensity weights mitigated the confounding influence of the observable characteristics.

The goal of propensity weights is for the weighted distribution of the observable variables in the comparison group to match the distribution for the group with the education credential

---

[6] It is likely that enlistees with the education credentials of interest differ from the comparison groups in ways that are not observed but that may affect the likelihood of attrition. For example, enlistees with homeschool diplomas may be more likely to come from rural areas, and this may be what is driving the difference between the groups. Another issue is that, because homeschoolers and distance learners were classified as Tier 2 during the period of our data, recruits having these credentials who were accessed during this time were most likely the best qualified from among the pool of applicants with these credentials. Therefore, attrition rates for these credentials may be biased downward compared to the entire pool of would-be accessions with these credentials.

[7] On doubly robust estimation, see Kang and Schafer, 2007. On propensity weights, see Rosenbaum and Rubin, 1983, and Hirano, Imbens, and Ridder, 2003.

[8] See Appendix B for a complete list of demographics included in the regressions as covariates.

[9] It is important to emphasize that, in this case, we are predicting the probability of being in the educational group of interest conditional on military service, cohort of entry, occupational code, AFQT score, race or ethnicity, and gender. We are not estimating the probability of being part of this group based on variables related to a family's decision to homeschool or to place their child in a distance learning school.

of interest.[10] We calculated the propensity weights for the comparison group members as the odds of being a recruit with a homeschool diploma and again as the odds of being a recruit with a distance learning diploma, e.g.:

$$\frac{Pr\left(\textit{recruit with homeschool diploma}\right)}{1-Pr\left(\textit{recruit with homeschool diploma}\right)}.$$

We took one additional step and performed a doubly robust analysis with a weighted logistic regression.[11] This doubly robust method offers an advantage over a simpler weighted comparison in that the propensity weights may not fully remove all confounding differences between the group with the education credential of interest and the comparison group. If small differences remain after weighting, the inclusion of the observable characteristics in the weighted logistic regression will control for any remaining confounding influence of differences in observable characteristics. We provide our results in Chapter Three, where we report average 12-, 24-, and 36-month attrition rates for the recruits with homeschool diplomas and for the counterfactual average predicted attrition rate for recruits with homeschool diplomas as if they were recruits with regular high school diplomas and as if they were recruits with GED credentials.[12] The difference between these two attrition rates (actual and counterfactual attrition rates for recruits with homeschool diplomas) is an estimate of the average effect of being a recruit with a homeschool diploma rather than one with a regular high school diploma. We also report the average 12-, 24-, and 36-month attrition rates for the recruits with homeschool diplomas and for the counterfactual average predicted attrition rate for recruits with homeschool diplomas as if they were recruits with a GED credential. The end result is to estimate whether differences in attrition rates are a function of the kind of education credential, holding other observable factors constant.

We conducted the same analyses for distance learning school diplomas by calculating the counterfactual average predicted attrition rate for recruits with distance learning school diplomas as if they were recruits with high school diplomas and as if they were recruits with GEDs.

---

10 Appendix B provides unweighted proportions and propensity weighted proportions for each control variable included in our regressions.

11 See Appendix C for the fully specified models used in the doubly robust regression analysis.

12 In this case the key assumption of the counterfactual framework is that each homeschool recruit has an observable outcome (attrition versus completion) as well as a potential but unobservable counterfactual outcome if they had instead been a regular high school diploma graduate (see Winship and Morgan, 1999).

CHAPTER THREE

Study Findings

The chapter includes our propensity weighted logistic analysis findings. For comparison purposes, we include results from the simple logistic regression models (i.e., without propensity weights or doubly robust estimation) in Appendix D.

Conceptual Overview

The analyses presented here are designed to estimate how holding a homeschool diploma or a distance learning diploma affects attrition outcomes. For each of the two of education credentials (homeschool and distance learning), we conducted the same series of analyses.

Using the homeschool diploma analysis for an example, we compared actual attrition rates for the people with a homeschool diploma to statistical estimates of their attrition rates (i.e., what we predict their attrition would look like) if they had received high school diplomas or GEDs instead. In this chapter, we first offer the comparison using the entire sample of homeschool diploma holders, without taking their AFQT scores into consideration. We then break the sample into two groups, those with AFQT scores greater than or equal to 50 and those below 50.

We separated the two AFQT groups to simulate the current breakout OSD uses to classify homeschool diploma holders into either Tier 1 or Tier 2. This allows us to examine whether the current policy of treating homeschool diploma holders differently based on the AFQT score grouping OSD has established is supported by the data. We include the calculations using the overall sample (i.e., without breaking it out by AFQT) to illustrate what would be observed if we had not taken into account the impact of AFQT.[1]

Overall, we found that breaking the data out into the two AFQT groups matters for homeschool diploma holders. That is, the patterns of predicted attrition differ depending on the AFQT group. Those who have AFQT scores of 50 or higher would be predicted to have attrition rates that would be only slightly lower than if they instead had high school diplomas. On a practical level, the differences are small—the predicted rates are 1 to 5 percentage points lower. However, for those with AFQT scores below 50, the effect of treating them as if they

[1] Note that, because we only examined the AFQT groupings OSD currently used, these analyses do not speak to revising the current system of tiering but only to how recruits with homeschool or distance learning diplomas should be treated within the current system, which categorizes applicants into tiers based on education credential and dichotomized AFQT scores.

had a high school diploma on their predicted attrition rates is larger and, on a practical level, is large enough to be of greater concern—the predicted rates are 6 to 11 percentage points lower.[2]

For distance learning school diploma holders, we found that breaking the data out by AFQT does not matter as much. Both AFQT groups—those 50 or higher and below 50—show sizable differences between their raw attrition rates and the predicted rates treating them as if they had received a high school diploma (5 to 7 percentage points lower for those with AFQT scores greater than 50 and predicted attrition rates that are 7 to 12 percentage points lower for those with AFQT scores less than 50). Thus, regardless of AFQT group, having a distance learning school diploma is associated with higher attrition.

Homeschool Diploma Comparisons

Table 3.1 shows the key results of our analyses for recruits with homeschool diplomas. The first row shows the observed 12-, 24-, and 36-month attrition rates for recruits with homeschool diplomas. The second row shows the estimate of their average attrition rate if, instead of a homeschool diploma, they had a regular high school diploma. Thus, the effect of being a recruit with a homeschool diploma relative to being a recruit with a regular high school diploma is an increase of 12-month attrition by 2 percentage points, 24-month attrition by 5 percentage points, and 36-month attrition by 6 percentage points. Similarly, the effect of being a recruit with a homeschool diploma rather than a GED is a decrease of 5 percentage points for 12-month and 24-month attrition and 7 percentage points for 36-month attrition. Put simply, after controlling for demographic differences, overall, recruits with homeschool degrees have attrition rates that lie between those of high school diploma holders and GED holders but that are closer to high school diploma holders than they are to GED holders.

Table 3.1 also displays the results of separate doubly robust analyses for recruits with AFQT scores greater than or equal to 50 and again for recruits with AFQT scores below 50. Note first that the results that are limited to recruits with AFQT scores greater than or equal to 50 show that recruits with homeschool diplomas have 12- and 24-month attrition rates within one or two percentage points of those of recruits with regular high school diplomas. This difference grows to 5 points for 36-month attrition. The results for recruits with AFQT scores below 50 are larger. For 12-month attrition, having a homeschool diploma instead of a regular high school diploma raises attrition rates by 6 percentage points. For 24-month attrition, having a homeschool diploma raises attrition rates by 10 percentage points. For 36-month attrition, having a homeschool diploma raises attrition rates by 11 percentage points. The effect of having a homeschool diploma relative to a GED is not statistically significant: Attrition rates for recruits with homeschool diplomas and AFQT scores below 50 are not different from those with GEDs.

[2] Because of our large sample sizes, differences could be statistically significant for many comparisons even if they are not practically significant (that is, if the difference is so small as to be irrelevant for treating the credentials differently). We also would expect slight variation in attrition rates due to chance alone. For that reason, we have focused our discussion and findings on the magnitude of the differences and make recommendations for policies on that basis.

Table 3.1
Doubly Robust Analysis of Attrition Rates for Recruits with Homeschool Diplomas

AFQT Category	Education Credential	12-Month Attrition	24-Month Attrition	36-Month Attrition
All AFQT scores	Homeschool diploma	17	26	33
	If homeschoolers had a high school diploma	15*	21*	27*
	If homeschoolers had a GED	22*	31*	40*
	High school comparison group N =	1,514,904	1,387,833	1,258,347
	GED comparison group N =	125,306	123,600	121,467
AFQT ≥ 50 (I to IIIA)	Homeschool diploma	15	22	30
	If homeschoolers had a high school diploma	14*	20*	25*
	If homeschoolers had a GED	21*	30*	38*
	High school comparison group N =	1,044,439	946,931	852,057
	GED comparison group N =	91,880	90,195	88,098
AFQT < 50 (IIIB to V)	Homeschool diploma	24	35	43
	If homeschoolers had a high school diploma	18*	25*	32*
	If homeschoolers had a GED	24	35	43
	High school comparison group N =	470,465	440,902	406,290
	GED comparison group N =	33,426	33,405	33,369

SOURCES: DMDC MEPCOM and Active Duty Military Personnel edit files.

NOTES: Table includes only non–prior service accessions. Twelve-month attrition includes FYs 2000–2011; 24-month attrition includes FYs 2000–2010; and 36-month attrition includes FYs 2000–2009. Services represented are Army, Navy, Marine Corps, Air Force, and Coast Guard. Even though AFQT categories range from I (AFQT > 92) to V (AFQT < 9), none of the homeschool diploma accessions had an AFQT score below category IVB (20 > AFQT > 15). Therefore, the bottom two categories dropped out of the regressions where populations with AFQT < 50 were included.

* Coefficient on homeschool was significant at the 0.05 level in the doubly robust regression.

Distance Learning School Diploma Comparisons

Table 3.2 shows the results of the analysis of distance learning school diplomas. These results suggest that distance learning school diplomas have even stronger negative effects on attrition than homeschool diplomas do. Including all AFQT categories in the analysis raised the effect of having a distance learning diploma relative to a regular high school diploma attrition rates by 5, 7, and 9 percentage points, respectively, for 12-month, 24-month, and 36-month attrition rates. The difference between recruits with distance learning school diplomas and GEDs is undetectable (meaning it was not significant at $p < 0.05$), except for 36-month attrition, where having a distance learning diploma rather than a GED lowers attrition rates by 3 percentage points. Restricting the analysis to recruits with AFQT scores of 50 or greater has similar results. However, for recruits with AFQT scores lower than 50, having a distance learning school diploma increases attrition rates by a factor of approximately 1.5 when compared to a regular high school diploma. For recruits with AFQT scores lower than 50, there is no discernible difference between holding a distance learning school diploma and a GED. Note that, although many of these differences are sizeable and likely stable, the sample size for distance learners (around 1,000) is noticeably smaller than those of other education credential groups in our data. For that reason, it would be prudent to conduct further research on these credentials when more data have been amassed.

Table 3.2
Doubly Robust Analysis of Attrition Rates for Recruits with Distance Learning School Diplomas

AFQT Category	Education Credential	12-Month Attrition	24-Month Attrition	36-Month Attrition
All AFQT scores	Distance learning school diploma	19	27	34
	If distance learners had a high school diploma	14*	20*	25*
	If distance learners had a GED	20	29	37*
	High school comparison group N =	1,507,602	1,381,155	1,252,330
	GED comparison group N =	118,132	117,044	115,561
AFQT ≥ 50 (I to IIIA)	Distance learning school diploma	19	26	32
	If distance learners had a high school diploma	14*	19*	25*
	If distance learners had a GED	20	29	37*
	High school comparison group N =	1,039,050	942,149	847,917
	GED comparison group N =	86,491	85,413	83,958
AFQT <50 (IIIB to V)	Distance learning school diploma	22	31	39
	If distance learners had a high school diploma	15*	21*	27*
	If distance learners had a GED	21	30	38
	High school comparison group N =	439,006	439,006	404,413
	GED comparison group N =	31,631	31,631	31,603

SOURCES: DMDC MEPCOM and Active Duty Military Personnel edit files.

NOTE: Table includes only non–prior service accessions. Twelve-month attrition includes FYs 2000–2011; 24-month attrition includes FYs 2000–2010; and 36-month attrition includes FYs 2000–2009. Services represented are Army, Navy, Marine Corps, Air Force, and Coast Guard. Even though AFQT categories range from I (AFQT > 92) to V (AFQT < 9), no distance learning diploma accessions had an AFQT score below category IVA (31 > AFQT > 20). Therefore, the bottom three categories dropped out of the regressions where populations with AFQT < 50 were included. As a reminder, although many of these differences are sizeable and likely stable, the sample size for distance learners (around 1,000) is noticeably smaller than those of other education credential groups in our data. For that reason, further research on these credentials would be prudent when more data has been amassed.

* Coefficient on homeschool was significant at the 0.05 level in the doubly robust regression.

CHAPTER FOUR

Conclusions and Recommendations

The goal of this effort was to determine whether applicants who scored less than 50 on the AFQT and have distance learning or homeschool credentials are more likely to attrit than those who scored less than 50 on the AFQT and have high school diplomas (all else being equal). According to our data, the answer is yes, they are more likely to attrit.

Holding a homeschool diploma instead of a regular high school diploma had significant negative effects on attrition rates. Overall, estimated attrition rates for recruits with homeschool diplomas are slightly, but statistically significantly, higher than attrition rates for recruits with regular high school diplomas. The negative effect of holding a homeschool diploma is larger for those with AFQT scores lower than 50. Holding a distance learning school diploma affected attrition more negatively than did holding a homeschool diploma, regardless of whether the recruit scored above 50 on the AFQT.

Although recruits with homeschool diplomas have 36-month attrition rates that are 5 points higher than recruits with regular high school diplomas, the small differences in 12- and 24-month attrition rates relative to the larger differences compared to GED holders convince us that these analyses support OSD's approach to treating recruits with homeschool diplomas who have AFQT scores greater than or equal to 50 the same as Tier 1 and treating recruits with homeschool diplomas and AFQT scores lower than 50 the same as Tier 2. Even with the noticeably smaller sample size, there is evidence to treat recruits with distance learning school diplomas the same as Tier 2, regardless of whether they are above or below 50 on the AFQT. However, as suggested previously, this group should be studied further as more data become available.

On the basis of these narrowly focused analyses, we recommend that OSD continue to use education credential for identifying applicants who are more likely to attrit. The current method of grouping education credentials predicts attrition better than not considering education credential at all. However, we cannot say, at this point, whether using a different system for grouping education credentials and AFQT scores into tiers would better predict attrition. Other options, such as using other cut scores on the AFQT and any ideas suggested by the external research literature, will be explored further in our next report.

Descriptive Statistics for Key Variables

The following figures and tables provide the distributions of the key variables of interest. Although our final tally of non–prior service regular service personnel was 1,999,459, the observation counts for the key variables of interest will not always be 1,999,459 because some observations have missing values for certain variables. In addition to these figures and tables, gender was recorded for 1,999,459 enlistees in our data set; of these, 336,299 (16.8 percent) were female.

Figure A.1
Distribution of Education Credentials at Time of Accession

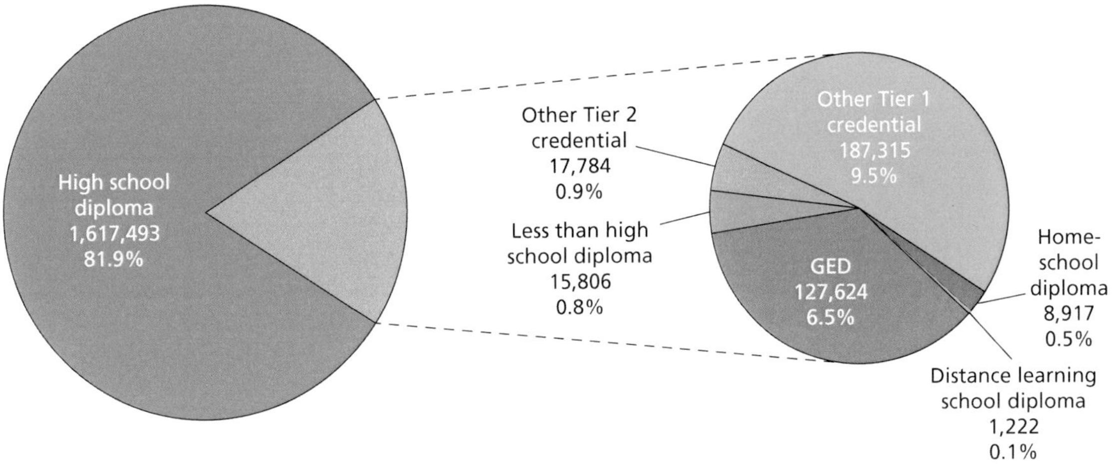

SOURCES: DMDC MEPCOM and Active Duty Military Personnel edit files.
NOTE: Values for accession education credential were present for 1,976,161 observations. Other Tier 1 credentials include some college, postsecondary school or greater, current high school senior, high school graduate who failed the exit exam, and adult education diploma. Other Tier 2 credentials include ChalleNGe GED, high school certificate of attendance, and occupational program.
RAND *RR374-A.1*

Figure A.2
Distribution of Service

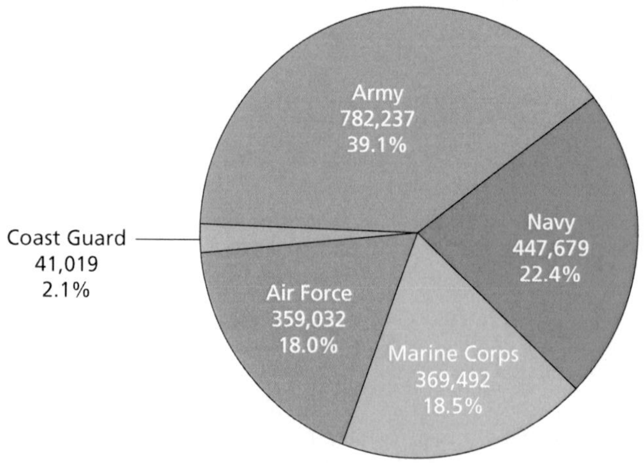

SOURCES: DMDC MEPCOM and Active Duty Military Personnel edit files.
NOTE: All 1,999,459 observations had a value for service branch.
RAND *RR374-A.2*

Figure A.3
Distribution of Race or Ethnicity

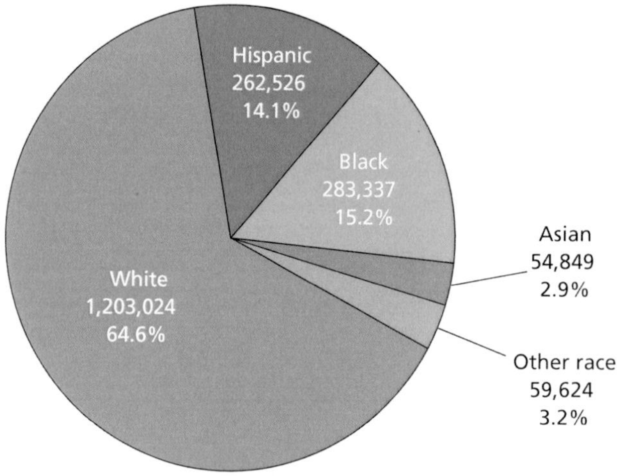

SOURCES: DMDC MEPCOM and Active Duty Military Personnel edit files.
NOTE: Values for race or ethnicity were present for 1,863,360 observations.
RAND *RR374-A.3*

Figure A.4
Distribution of Accession AFQT Category Code

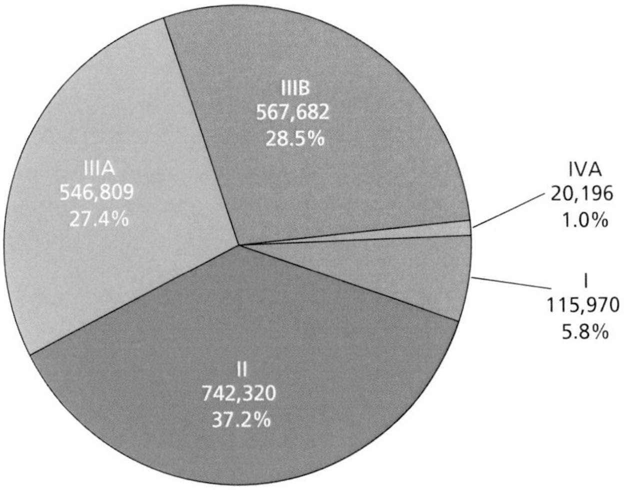

SOURCES: DMDC MEPCOM and Active Duty Military Personnel edit files.
NOTE: Values for accession AFQT were present for 1,993,309 observations. AFQT category I is an AFQT score > 92, category II is a score greater than 64, category IIIA is a score greater than 49, category IIIB is a score greater than 30, and category IVA is a score greater than 20. Not shown in the figure are 181 observations with an AFQT Category IVB (20 ≥ AFQT ≥ 16), 139 observations with an AFQT category IVC (15 ≥ AFQT ≥ 10), and 12 observations with an AFQT category V (AFQT < 10). These three categories sum to less than 0.0 percent of observations.
RAND *RR374-A.4*

Figure A.5
Distribution of Duty DoD Occupation Code

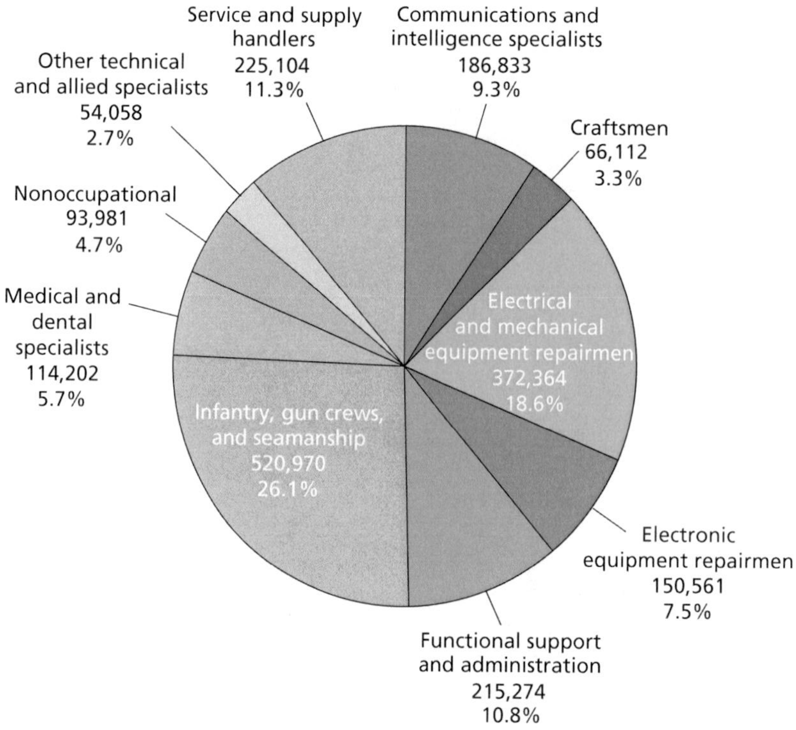

SOURCES: DMDC MEPCOM and Active Duty Military Personnel edit files.
NOTE: All 1,999,459 observations had a value for Duty DoD Occupation Code.
RAND *RR374-A.5*

Table A.1
Raw Attrition Rates by Service and Entry Cohort FYs

Entry Cohort FYs	12-Month Attrition (%)					24-Month Attrition (%)					36-Month Attrition (%)				
	Army	Navy	Marine Corps	Air Force	Coast Guard	Army	Navy	Marine Corps	Air Force	Coast Guard	Army	Navy	Marine Corps	Air Force	Coast Guard
2000	15	18	14	12	13	25	25	19	17	23	36	30	24	21	27
2001	17	17	14	8	12	26	24	19	13	20	33	29	23	17	24
2002	17	13	15	9	10	24	20	18	13	16	32	27	23	23	21
2003	17	13	12	9	10	24	21	16	16	16	32	27	20	24	21
2004	19	12	12	13	10	26	19	16	19	15	32	26	20	24	21
2005	15	12	13	12	10	23	19	18	17	15	29	25	21	22	19
2006	11	13	13	12	10	20	20	17	17	16	27	24	21	21	20
2007	14	15	13	15	9	22	20	17	19	13	29	25	20	23	18
2008	15	15	11	12	8	22	20	15	16	13	29	25	20	22	20
2009	14	12	11	9	8	20	17	15	14	15	28	23	19	21	19
2010	12	10	9	11	8	18	14	12	15	11	—	—	—	—	—
2011	12	11	8	10	7	—	—	—	—	—	—	—	—	—	—

SOURCES: DMDC MEPCOM and Active Duty Military Personnel edit files.

Table A.2
Percentage of Enlistees with AFQT ≥ 50 (I to IIIA) by Service and Entry Cohort FYs

Entry Cohort FYs	Army	Navy	Marine Corps	Air Force	Coast Guard
2000	65	64	64	73	77
2001	64	63	65	75	78
2002	70	65	67	76	77
2003	72	66	69	81	77
2004	72	69	70	82	79
2005	68	69	68	82	76
2006	61	73	68	79	75
2007	61	72	65	79	81
2008	62	73	66	80	85
2009	66	78	69	81	92
2010	64	83	72	91	95
2011	63	89	74	99	95

SOURCES: DMDC MEPCOM and Active Duty Military Personnel edit files.

Table A.3
Distribution of Accession Education Credential by AFQT Category Code
Accessions Without a Waiver For "Mental Qualification—Meets ASVAB Testing Requirements"

AFQT Category Code	High School Diploma (%)	Homeschool Diploma (%)	Distance Learning School Diploma (%)	GED (%)	Less than High School Diploma (%)	Other Tier 1 Credential (%)	Other Tier 2 Credential (%)
I (AFQT > 92)	5.1	6.4	4.0	1.7	1.7	15.0	1.2
II (92 ≥ AFQT≥65)	37.3	40.6	37.1	32.4	34.6	41.7	20.8
IIIA (64 ≥ AFQT≥50)	27.1	28.9	38.8	40.1	51.2	20.4	28.7
IIIB (49 ≥ AFQT≥31)	29.4	23.7	19.8	25.7	12.4	22.1	47.2
IVA (30 ≥ AFQT≥21)	1.1	0.5	0.2	0.1	0.0	0.9	2.1
IVB (20 ≥ AFQT≥16)	0.0	0.0	0.0	0.0	0.0	0.0	0.0
IVC (15 ≥ AFQT≥10)	0.0	0.0	0.0	0.0	0.0	0.0	0.0
V (AFQT < 10)	0.0	0.0	0.0	0.0	0.0	0.0	0.0

SOURCES: DMDC MEPCOM and Active Duty Military Personnel edit files.

NOTE: Other Tier 1 credentials include some college, postsecondary school or greater, current high school senior, high school graduate who failed the exit exam, and adult education diploma. Other Tier 2 credentials include ChalleNGe GED, high school certificate of attendance, and occupational program.

APPENDIX B

Effectiveness of the Propensity Weights

As discussed in Chapter Two, the goal of propensity weights is for the weighted distribution of the observable variables in the comparison group to match the distribution for the group with the education credential of interest. Tables B.1 through B.3 below provide means of the regression covariates for the homeschooled population and both the unweighted and weighted means using the calculated propensity scores for the high school and GED recipient populations. Table B.1 is for the entire FY 2000–2011 population of non–prior service accessions. Table B.2 is for the population with AFQT scores ≥ 50, and Table B.3 is for the population with AFQT scores < 50. In each case, the unweighted populations of traditional high school graduates and GED recipients look different from the population of homeschool diploma recipients. However, when the covariates are adjusted using the propensity scores, the means for these populations look very similar to those for the homeschooled population. In Tables B.1 through B.3, small yet significant differences remain in the distribution across service branches when comparing the homeschool diploma population to the weighted GED recipient population. Additionally, small yet significant differences remain in the distribution across cohorts when comparing the homeschool diploma population to the weighted GED recipient population in Table B.3.

Tables B.4 through B.6 provide the means of the regression covariates for the distance learning school population and both the unweighted and weighted means using the calculated propensity scores for the high school and GED recipient populations. Table B.4 is for the entire FY 2000–2011 population of non–prior service accessions. Table B.5 is for the population with AFQT scores ≥ 50, and Table B.6 is for the population with AFQT scores < 50. In each case, the unweighted populations of traditional high school graduates and GED recipients look different from the population of distance learning school diploma recipients. However, when the covariates are adjusted using the propensity scores, the means for these populations look very similar to those for the distance learning school population.

Table B.1
Unweighted Versus Propensity Weighted Percentages for All AFQT Scores, Homeschool

Covariate	Homeschool (%)	High School (%)		GED (%)	
		Unweighted	Weighted	Unweighted	Weighted
Service					
Army	44	33*	44	80*	44
Navy	20	24*	20	12*	21*
Marine Corps	28	21*	28	5*	26*
Air Force	7	20*	7	1*	8*
Coast Guard	1	2*	1	2*	1
Career					
Communications and intelligence specialists	10	9*	10	9*	10
Craftsmen	3	3*	3	3	3
Electrical and mechanical equipment repairmen	16	19*	16	17	16
Electronic equipment repairmen	7	8*	7	7	7
Functional support and administration	7	11*	7	8*	7
Infantry, gun crews, and seamanship specialists	38	25*	38	37*	37
Medical and dental specialists	4	6*	4	4*	4
Nonoccupational	4	5	4	3*	5
Other technical and allied specialists	2	3*	2	2	2
Service and supply handlers	10	12*	10	10*	10
Entry cohort FY					
2000	9	10*	9	10*	9
2001	10	10	10	12*	10
2002	8	10*	8	10*	8
2003	2	4*	2	3*	2
2004	9	9	9	7*	9
2005	8	8	8	8*	8
2006	8	8	8	13*	8
2007	10	8*	10	14*	10
2008	11	8*	11	13*	11
2009	10	8*	10	6*	9
2010	9	9	9	1*	8
2011	8	8	8	1*	8
AFQT category					
I	6	5*	6	2*	7
II	41	37*	41	32*	41
IIIA	29	27*	29	40*	28
IIIB	24	30*	24	27*	24
IVA	1	1*	1	0*	1

Table B.1—Continued

Covariate	Homeschool (%)	High School (%)		GED (%)	
		Unweighted	Weighted	Unweighted	Weighted
IVB	0	0	0	0	0
IVC	0	0*	0*	0	0*
V	0	0*	0*	0	0
Race or ethnicity					
White	86	64*	86	76*	86
Hispanic	6	14*	6	10*	6
Black	5	16*	5	10*	5
Asian	1	3*	1	1*	1
Other	3	3*	3	2	3
Gender					
Female	12	17*	12	11*	13

SOURCES: DMDC MEPCOM and Active Duty Military Personnel edit files.

NOTE: * indicates a significant ($p < 0.05$) difference from the homeschool proportion.

Table B.2
Unweighted Versus Propensity Weighted Percentages for AFQT Scores >= 50 (I to IIIA), Homeschool

Covariate	Homeschool (%)	High School (%)		GED (%)	
		Unweighted	Weighted	Unweighted	Weighted
Service					
Army	41	29*	41	75*	41
Navy	19	24*	19	16*	21*
Marine Corps	32	21*	32	6*	28*
Air Force	8	24*	8	1*	10*
Coast Guard	1	2*	1	2*	1
Career					
Communications and intelligence specialists	11	11	11	10*	11
Craftsmen	2	3*	2	3*	2
Electrical and mechanical equipment repairmen	15	20*	15	17*	15
Electronic equipment repairmen	8	10*	8	8	8
Functional support and administration	6	10*	6	7*	6
Infantry, gun crews, and seamanship specialists	37	23*	37	35*	36
Medical and dental specialists	5	7*	5	6*	5
Nonoccupational	4	5*	4	3*	5
Other technical and allied specialists	2	3*	2	2	2
Service and supply handlers	8	9	8	9	8

Table B.2—Continued

Covariate	Homeschool (%)	High School (%)		GED (%)	
		Unweighted	Weighted	Unweighted	Weighted
Entry cohort FY					
2000	7	9*	7	12*	7
2001	8	9*	8	12*	8
2002	7	9*	7	12*	7
2003	2	4*	2	4*	2
2004	8	10*	8	8	9
2005	7	8	7	7	8
2006	7	8*	7	11*	7
2007	10	8*	10	12*	10
2008	12	8*	12	12	12
2009	12	9*	12	7*	11
2010	11	9*	11	2*	11
2011	10	9*	10	1*	9
AFQT category					
I	8	7*	8	2*	9
II	54	54	54	43*	54
IIIA	38	39	38	54*	37
Race or ethnicity					
White	88	70*	88	79*	88
Hispanic	5	12*	5	9*	5
Black	3	12*	3	8*	3
Asian	1	3*	1	1*	1
Other	3	3*	3	3	3
Gender					
Female	12	16*	12	10*	12

SOURCES: DMDC MEPCOM and Active Duty Military Personnel edit files.

NOTE: * indicates a significant ($p < 0.05$) difference from the homeschool proportion.

Table B.3
Unweighted Versus Propensity Weighted Percentages for AFQT Scores < 50 (IIIB to V), Homeschool

Covariate	Homeschool (%)	High School (%)		GED (%)	
		Unweighted	Weighted	Unweighted	Weighted
Service					
Army	55	40*	55	93*	52*
Navy	22	24	22	1*	26*
Marine Corps	18	22*	18	5*	17
Air Force	4	13*	4	0*	4
Coast Guard	0	1*	0	1*	0
Career					

Table B.3—Continued

Covariate	Homeschool (%)	High School (%)		GED (%)	
		Unweighted	Weighted	Unweighted	Weighted
Communications and intelligence specialists	6	5	6	7*	6
Craftsmen	4	4	4	4	3
Electrical and mechanical equipment repairmen	18	19	18	15*	19
Electronic equipment repairmen	2	2	2	3*	2
Functional support and administration	8	13*	8	9	9
Infantry, gun crews, and seamanship specialists	40	29*	40	40	40
Medical and dental specialists	1	3*	1	1	1
Nonoccupational	5	4	5	3*	4
Other technical and allied specialists	1	2	1	3*	1
Service and supply handlers	14	18*	14	15	14
Entry cohort FY					
2000	15	11*	15	7*	13*
2001	17	11*	17	13*	13*
2002	10	10	10	5*	11
2003	3	5*	3	1*	5*
2004	11	9*	11	4*	14*
2005	10	8*	10	11	9
2006	11	8*	11	20*	10
2007	10	8*	10	21*	10
2008	9	9	9	17*	9
2009	3	8*	3	3	3
2010	1	7*	1	0*	1
2011	1	6*	1	0*	2
AFQT category					
IIIB	98	96*	98	100*	97
IVA	2	4*	2	0*	3
IVB	0	0	0	0	0
IVC	0	0*	0*	0	0*
V	0	0*	0*	0*	0*
Race or ethnicity					
White	80	50*	80	69*	80
Hispanic	8	19*	8	13*	8
Black	9	25*	9	15*	9
Asian	1	3*	1	1*	1
Other	2	3*	2	2	2

Table B.3—Continued

Covariate	Homeschool (%)	High School (%)		GED (%)	
		Unweighted	Weighted	Unweighted	Weighted
Gender					
Female	13	20*	13	12	14

SOURCES: DMDC MEPCOM and Active Duty Military Personnel edit files.

NOTE: * indicates a significant ($p < 0.05$) difference from the homeschool proportion.

Table B.4
Unweighted Versus Propensity Weighted Percentages for All AFQT Scores, Distance Learning

Covariate	Distance Learning School (%)	High School (%)		GED (%)	
		Unweighted	Weighted	Unweighted	Weighted
Service					
Army	32	33	32	80*	32
Navy	42	24*	42	12*	42
Marine Corps	25	21*	25	5*	25
Air Force	2	20*	2	1	2
Coast Guard	1	2*	1	2*	1
Career					
Communications and intelligence specialists	9	9	9	9	9
Craftsmen	4	3	4	3	4
Electrical and mechanical equipment repairmen	20	19	20	17*	20
Electronic equipment repairmen	8	8	8	7	8
Functional support and administration	8	11*	8	8	8
Infantry, gun crews, and seamanship specialists	32	25*	32	37*	32
Medical and dental specialists	5	6	5	4	5
Nonoccupational	2	5*	2	3	2
Other technical and allied specialists	2	3	2	2	2
Service and supply handlers	10	12	10	10	10
Entry cohort FY					
2000	3	10*	3	10*	3
2001	4	10*	4	12*	4
2002	6	10*	6	10*	6
2003	2	4*	2	3	2
2004	7	9*	7	7	7
2005	8	8	8	8	8
2006	12	8*	12	13	12
2007	17	8*	17	14*	17

Table B.4—Continued

Covariate	Distance Learning School (%)	High School (%)		GED (%)	
		Unweighted	Weighted	Unweighted	Weighted
2008	21	8*	21	13*	21
2009	10	8*	10	6*	10
2010	5	9*	5	1*	5
2011	4	8*	4	1*	4
AFQT category					
I	4	5	4	2*	4
II	37	37	37	32*	37
IIIA	39	27*	39	40	39
IIIB	20	30*	20	27*	20
IVA	0	1*	0	0	0
IVB	0	0*	0*	0*	0*
IVC	0	0*	0*	0	0*
V	0	0*	0*	0	0
Race or ethnicity					
White	72	64*	72	76*	72
Hispanic	12	14*	12	10	12
Black	10	16*	10	10	10
Asian	2	3*	2	1	2
Other	4	3	4	2*	4
Gender					
Female	14	17*	14	11*	14

SOURCES: DMDC MEPCOM and Active Duty Military Personnel edit files.

NOTE: * indicates a significant ($p < 0.05$) difference from the distance learning school proportion.

Table B.5
Unweighted Versus Propensity Weighted Percentages for AFQT Scores >= 50 (I to IIIA), Distance Learning

Covariate	Distance Learning School (%)	High School (%)		GED (%)	
		Unweighted	Weighted	Unweighted	Weighted
Service					
Army	27	29	27	75*	27
Navy	50	24*	50	16*	51
Marine Corps	21	21	21	6*	21
Air Force	1	24*	1	1	1
Coast Guard	1	2*	1	2*	1
Career					
Communications and intelligence specialists	10	11	10	10	10
Craftsmen	4	3	4	3	4

Table B.5—Continued

Covariate	Distance Learning School (%)	High School (%)		GED (%)	
		Unweighted	Weighted	Unweighted	Weighted
Electrical and mechanical equipment repairmen	20	20	20	17*	20
Electronic equipment repairmen	10	10	10	8	10
Functional support and administration	8	10	8	7	8
Infantry, gun crews, and seamanship specialists	29	23*	29	35*	29
Medical and dental specialists	6	7	6	6	6
Nonoccupational	2	5*	2	3	2
Other technical and allied specialists	2	3	2	2	2
Service and supply handlers	8	9	8	9	7
Entry cohort FY					
2000	3	9*	3	12*	3
2001	5	9*	5	12*	5
2002	6	9*	6	12*	6
2003	3	4	3	4*	3
2004	8	10*	8	8	7
2005	7	8	7	7	7
2006	10	8*	10	11	10
2007	16	8*	16	12*	16
2008	20	8*	20	12*	20
2009	12	9*	12	7*	12
2010	6	9*	6	2*	6
2011	5	9*	5	1*	5
AFQT category					
I	5	7*	5	2*	5
II	46	54*	46	43	46
IIIA	49	39*	49	54*	49
Race or ethnicity					
White	73	70*	73	79*	73
Hispanic	12	12	12	9*	12
Black	9	12*	9	8	9
Asian	2	3*	2	1	2
Other	4	3	4	3*	4
Gender					
Female	15	16	15	10*	15

SOURCES: DMDC MEPCOM and Active Duty Military Personnel edit files.

NOTE: * indicates a significant ($p < 0.05$) difference from the distance learning school proportion.

Table B.6
Unweighted Versus Propensity Weighted Percentages for AFQT Scores < 50 (IIIB to V), Distance Learning

Covariate	Distance Learning School (%)	High School (%)		GED (%)	
		Unweighted	Weighted	Unweighted	Weighted
Service					
Army	50	40*	50	93*	50
Navy	7	24*	7	1*	7
Marine Corps	41	22*	41	5*	40
Air Force	3	13*	3	0*	3
Coast Guard	0	1*	0	1*	0
Career					
Communications and intelligence specialists	5	5	5	7	5
Craftsmen	4	4	4	4	4
Electrical and mechanical equipment repairmen	16	19	16	15	17
Electronic equipment repairmen	1	2	1	3*	1
Functional support and administration	8	13*	8	9	8
Infantry, gun crews, and seamanship specialists	40	29*	40	40	40
Medical and dental specialists	0	3*	0	1	0
Nonoccupational	3	4	3	3	3
Other technical and allied specialists	2	2	2	3	2
Service and supply handlers	19	18	19	15	20
Entry cohort FY					
2000	5	11*	5	7	5
2001	4	11*	4	13*	4
2002	3	10*	3	5*	3
2003	0	5*	0	1	0
2004	5	9*	5	4	5
2005	9	8	9	11	9
2006	16	8*	16	20	16
2007	22	8*	22	21	22
2008	27	9*	27	17*	27
2009	6	8	6	3*	6
2010	2	7*	2	0*	2
2011	0	6*	0*	0*	0*
AFQT category					
IIIB	99	96*	99	100	99
IVA	1	4*	1	0	1

Table B.6—Continued

Covariate	Distance Learning School (%)	High School (%)		GED (%)	
		Unweighted	Weighted	Unweighted	Weighted
IVB	0	0*	0*	0*	0*
IVC	0	0*	0*	0	0*
V	0	0*	0*	0*	0*
Race or ethnicity					
White	68	50*	68	69	69
Hispanic	13	19*	13	13	13
Black	14	25*	14	15	15
Asian	2	3	2	1	2
Other	3	3	3	2	2
Gender					
Female	12	20*	12	12	12

SOURCES: DMDC MEPCOM and Active Duty Military Personnel edit files.

NOTE: * indicates a significant ($p < 0.05$) difference from the distance learner proportion.

Models Used in Doubly Robust Regression Analysis

We performed our doubly robust regression analysis for the four education credentials of interest and comparison group combinations shown in Table C.1. We ran a separate set of regressions using only the subset of the sample that is relevant to the comparison (i.e., individuals who did not get the education credential of interest or the comparison credential are not included in that regression).

For each education credential of interest and comparison group combination, we first computed a propensity score for each member of the comparison group using a logistic regression:

$$\begin{aligned} \textit{Education Credential}_i = \beta_1 + \beta_2 \textit{Service}_i + \beta_3 \textit{Cohort}_i \\ + \beta_4 \textit{Duty}_i + \beta_5 \textit{AFQT}_i + \beta_6 \textit{Race}_i + \beta_7 \textit{Female}_i + \varepsilon_i, \end{aligned}$$

where *Education Credential* is an indicator variable equal to 0 if enlistee i is part of the comparison group and equal to 1 if enlistee i is part of the group with the education credential of interest. *Service* is a vector of indicator variables for each regular branch of the armed services; *Cohort* is a vector of indicator variables for each active federal military service entry FY 2000–2011; *Duty* is a vector of indicator variables for each two-digit duty occupation code; *AFQT* is a vector of indicator variables for each AFQT category; *Race* is a vector of indicator variables for each race or ethnicity; and *Female* is an indicator variable equal to one if the enlistee is female. ε is an idiosyncratic error term.

The predictions from these logistic regression models create the propensity scores. We calculated the propensity weights for the comparison group members as the odds of being a recruit from the group with the education credential of interest:

$$\frac{Pr(\textit{recruit from group with eduction credential of interest})}{1 - Pr(\textit{recruit from group with eduction credential of interest})}.$$

Table C.1
Education Credential of Interest and Comparison Group Matrix for Doubly Robust Regressions

Regression	Education Credential of Interest	Comparison Group
1	Homeschool Diploma	High School Diploma
2	Homeschool Diploma	GED
3	Distance Learning School Diploma	High School Diploma
4	Distance Learning School Diploma	GED

We assigned members of the group with the education credential of interest a weight equal to 1, then we ran a weighted logistic regression predicting attrition using the propensity weights:

$$Attrit_{ij} = \delta_1 + \omega Education\ Credential_i W_i + \delta_2 Service_i W_i + \delta_3 Cohort_i W_i + \delta_4 Duty_i W_i + \delta_5 AFQT_i W_i + \delta_6 Race_i W_i + \delta_7 Female_i W_i + \mu_i,$$

where *Attrit* is an indicator variable equal to 0 if enlistee *i* remains in the armed services for length of time *j* and equal to 1 if enlistee *i* attrits within length of time *j*. We ran separate models for each length of time of interest (i.e., *j* = 12 months, *j* = 24 months, and *j* = 36 months). We also ran separate models for each education credential comparison, where *Education Credential* is an indicator variable equal to 0 if enlistee *i* is part of the comparison group and equal to 1 if enlistee *i* is part of the group with the education credential of interest; *Service* is a vector of indicator variables for each regular branch of the armed services; *Cohort* is a vector of indicator variables for each active federal military service entry year 2000–2011; *Duty* is a vector of indicator variables for each two-digit duty occupation code; *AFQT* is a vector of indicator variables for each AFQT category code; *Race* is a vector of indicator variables for each race or ethnicity; and *Female* is an indicator variable equal to one if the enlistee is female. In our weighted logistic regression, each covariate is multiplied by the weight (W_i) that was calculated for each enlistee *i* using the process described above. The remaining component, μ, is an idiosyncratic error term.

We repeated this same set of analyses limiting the data to those with AFQT scores greater than or equal to 50 and again for those with AFQT scores less than 50.

Simple Logistic Regression Model

In addition to performing a doubly robust estimation including propensity weights and regression, we also examined attrition rates using a more-traditional approach for comparison purposes. We did this for the same four education credentials of interest and comparison group combinations described earlier, in Table C.1. This appendix describes the results of that approach.

We first ran a simple logistic regression using the demographic variables and education credential to predict 12-, 24-, and 36-month attrition:

$$Attrit_{ij} = \delta_1 + \omega Education\ Credential_i + \delta_2 Service_i + \delta_3 Cohort_i$$
$$+ \delta_4 Duty_i + \delta_5 AFQT_i + \delta_6 Race_i + \delta_7 Female_i + \mu_i,$$

where *Attrit* is an indicator variable equal to 0 if enlistee *i* remains in the armed services for length of time *j* and equal to 1 if enlistee *i* attrits within length of time *j*. We ran separate models for each length of time of interest (i.e., j = 12 months, j = 24 months, and j = 36 months). We also ran separate models for each education credential comparison, where *Education Credential* is an indicator variable equal to 0 if enlistee *i* is part of the comparison group and equal to 1 if enlistee *i* is part of the group with the education credential of interest.[1] *Service* is a vector of indicator variables for each regular branch of the armed services; *Cohort* is a vector of indicator variables for each active federal military service entry FY 2000–2011; *Duty* is a vector of indicator variables for each two-digit duty occupation code; *AFQT* is a vector of indicator variables for each AFQT category code; *Race* is a vector of indicator variables for each race or ethnicity; and *Female* is an indicator variable equal to one if the enlistee is female. μ is an idiosyncratic error term.

We then used the resulting logistic regression model weights to create a predicted probability of attrition for each homeschooler as if he or she had instead received a high school diploma, by switching only the values in the regression model corresponding to the education credential dummy variable. For example, the second row in Table D.1 shows the average predicted probability of attrition for homeschoolers when the dummy variable for high school is

[1] For each attrition outcome (j = 12 months, j = 24 months, and j = 36 months) we ran four separate regressions. Homeschool credentials are compared to each of the other two education credentials separately (first high school and second GED) and distance learning is compared to each of the other two education credentials separately (first high school and second GED). For example, in the homeschool/high school regression comparison the *Education Credential* indicator variable is coded as follows: homeschool (the education credential of interest) = 1, high school (the comparison group) = 0, and all other education credential holders (e.g., GEDs, distance learners, etc.,) are set to missing and dropped from the regression.

set equal to 1 and the dummy variable for homeschool is set to zero. We repeated these analyses limiting the data to those with AFQT scores greater than or equal to 50 and again for the subset of enlistees with AFQT scores less than 50.

Tables D.1 and D.2 display the results of this analysis for recruits with homeschool diplomas and with distance learning school diplomas respectively.

Table D.1
Regression Adjusted Attrition Rates for Recruits with Homeschool Diplomas

AFQT Category	Education Credential	12-Month Attrition	24-Month Attrition	36-Month Attrition
All AFQT scores	Homeschool diploma	17	26	33
	If homeschoolers had a high school diploma	15*	22*	28*
	If homeschoolers had a GED	22*	31*	40*
	High school comparison group N =	1,514,997	1,387,918	1,258,415
	GED comparison group N =	125,307	123,601	121,468
AFQT ≥ 50 (I to IIIA)	Homeschool diploma	15	22	30
	If homeschoolers had a high school diploma	14*	20*	26*
	If homeschoolers had a GED	21*	29*	38*
	High school comparison group N =	1,044,439	946,931	852,057
	GED comparison group N =	91,880	90,195	88,098
AFQT < 50 (IIIB to V)	Homeschool diploma	24	35	43
	If homeschoolers had a high school diploma	18*	26*	33*
	If homeschoolers had a GED	25	36	45
	High school comparison group N =	470,558	440,987	406,358
	GED comparison group N =	33,427	33,406	33,370

SOURCES: DMDC MEPCOM and Active Duty Military Personnel edit files.

NOTES: Table includes only non–prior service accessions. Twelve-month attrition includes FYs 2000–2011; 24-month attrition includes FYs 2000–2010; and 36-month attrition includes FYs 2000–2009. Services represented are Army, Navy, Marine Corps, Air Force, and Coast Guard.

* Coefficient on homeschool was significant at the 0.05 level in the logistic regression.

Table D.2
Regression Adjusted Attrition Rates for Recruits with Distance Learning School Diplomas

AFQT Category	Education Credential	12-Month Attrition	24-Month Attrition	36-Month Attrition
All AFQT scores	Distance learning school diploma	19	27	34
	If distance learners had a high school diploma	14*	20*	25*
	If distance learners had a GED	22*	31*	39*
	High school comparison group N =	1,507,827	1,381,366	1,252,513
	GED comparison group N =	118,137	117,049	115,566
AFQT ≥ 50 (I to IIIA)	Distance learning school diploma	19	26	32
	If distance learners had a high school diploma	14*	20*	25*
	If distance learners had a GED	22*	31*	38*
	High school comparison group N =	1,039,050	942,149	847,917
	GED comparison group N =	86,491	85,413	83,958
AFQT < 50 (IIIB to V)	Distance learning school diploma	22	31	39
	If distance learners had a high school diploma	16*	22*	28*
	If distance learners had a GED	21	31	39
	High school comparison group N =	468,777	439,217	404,596
	GED comparison group N =	31,646	31,636	31,608

SOURCES: DMDC MEPCOM and Active Duty Military Personnel edit files.

NOTE: Table includes only non–prior service accessions. Twelve-month attrition includes FYs 2000–2011; 24-month attrition includes FYs 2000–2010; and 36-month attrition includes FYs 2000–2009. Services represented are Army, Navy, Marine Corps, Air Force, and Coast Guard. As a reminder, although many of these differences are sizable and likely stable, the sample size for distance learners (around 1,000) is noticeably smaller than that of other education credential groups in our data. For that reason, further research on these credentials would be prudent once more data have been amassed.

* Coefficient on homeschool was significant at the 0.05 level in the logistic regression.

References

Hirano, Keisuke, Guido W. Imbens, and Geert Ridder, "Efficient Estimation of Average Treatment Effects Using the Estimated Propensity Score," *Econometrica*, Vol. 71, No. 4, 2003, pp. 1161–1189.

House Resolution 1540, National Defense Authorization Act for Fiscal Year 2012.

Kang, Joseph D., and Joseph L. Schafer, "Demystifying Double Robustness," *Statistical Science,* Vol. 22, No. 4, 2007, pp. 523–539.

Rosenbaum, Paul R., and Donald B. Rubin, "The Central Role of the Propensity Score in Observational Studies for Causal Effects," *Biometrika*, Vol. 70, No. 1, 1983, pp. 41–55.

Vollrath, Frederick, Office of the Under Secretary of Defense (Personnel and Readiness) memorandum, "Education Credentials—Definition and Tier Placement," memorandum for Assistant Secretary of Army (Manpower and Reserve Affairs), Assistant Secretary of Navy (Manpower and Reserve Affairs), Assistant Secretary of Air Force (Manpower, Reserve Affairs, Installations, and Environment), Washington, D.C., June 6, 2012.

Winship, Christopher, and Stephen L. Morgan, "The Estimation of Causal Effects from Observational Data," *Annual Review of Sociology,* Vol. 25, 1999, pp. 659–707.